The Employer's Handbook:
Sexual Harassment in the Workplace

Written by
Ryan Jacobson

Edited by
Cathy Caligiuri

The Employer's Handbook: Sexual Harassment in the Workplace

Copyright 2016

Printed in the United States of America

Published by SM&DS through Createspace Independent Publishing Platform

ISBN-13: 978-1530707263

ISBN-10: 1530707269

Table of Contents

About the Book

Sexual Harassment is perhaps the most pervasive, controversial, and detrimental behavior in the workplace that is extremely costly for employees and employers. Especially in male-dominated fields, reported and unreported incidents of sexual harassment have been shown to cost organizations billions of dollars every year through lowered employee job performance, increased turn-over rate of employees, and reduced team performance. The purpose of this book is to shed light on the causes, antecedents, and consequences of sexual harassment in the workplace.

This book includes a brief history of the causes of sexual harassment in male-dominated fields, explains the legal implications for employers, and includes specific policy suggestions for employers to follow. Employers that work in male-dominated fields, particularly STEM (science, technology, engineering, and math) will find this book to be an invaluable resource for creating effective sexual harassment policies in their organization. It will help them understand the prevalence of sexual harassment in male-dominated fields, the different types of sexual harassment, gender differences in perceptions of sexual harassment, employer liability for Sexual Harassment under the Equal Employment Opportunity Commission

(EEOC), the legal definition of sexual harassment, and Quid Pro Quo vs. Hostile Environment Harassment.

This book also has practical policy suggestions for employers based on EEOC guidelines, a brief review of the causes of gender discrimination in the workplace from a system justification perspective, lists of specific sexual harassment scenarios that could constitute as illegal in the workplace, questions that are commonly used in court to determine if the behavior was sexual harassment, and a brief summary of what to expect when a complaint is filed to the EEOC.

Introduction

As women enter traditionally masculine-dominated domains, men may feel that their exclusive access to such domains and the benefits that are associated with them are being threatened (Berdahl & Raver, 2012). As a result, men may attempt to mitigate female leadership because men in general possess higher societal status than women, and might view any women who attempted to gain influence in a traditionally male-dominated domain as a threat competing for resources, power, and social authority (Eagly & Carli, 2007). For example, research has demonstrated that men tend to show more disapproval of high levels of female competence than high levels of male competence, and exhibit greater resistance toward women's influence than women do (Carli, 2004; Eagly & Carli, 2007). Men may be more likely to display increased resistance to women seeking to advance into higher level leadership positions and in roles typically held by men associated with high societal status because more power and influence are at stake (Eagly & Carli, 2007). In highly influential traditionally male-dominated positions of leadership, women often represent a small numerical minority, which has been associated with increased negative reactions towards women seeking advancement such as ignoring ideas and increased negative reactions toward self-promoting behaviors (Chatman et al., 2005). However, one of the most severe and prevalent ways men attempt to obstruct women from advancing to leadership positions and entering traditionally male-dominated domains is through sexual harassment.

Perhaps the most pervasive, detrimental, and harmful obstacle obstructing the advancement of women in Science, Technology, Engineering, and Math (STEM) fields is the occurrence of sexual harassment in the workplace. Women entering into STEM related fields are not only vastly outnumbered by men, they are also subjected to an extremely high rate of sexual harassment. One survey of over 600 female scientists found that nearly two thirds experienced some form of sexual harassment (Hyde, Nelson, College, & Rutherford, 2014). Additionally, nearly 20% of female scientists reported that they experienced sexual assault or unwanted physical sexual contact (Hyde, Nelson, College, & Rutherford, 2014). Thus, females in STEM experience a difficult, potentially dangerous, work environment that may discourage women from entering into science and math related fields (Zadronzy, 2014). Additionally, the negative psychological and job related impact that often result from being harassed at work could be one possible reason why so few women persist in STEM fields (Hyde, Nelson, College, & Rutherford, 2014; Zadronzy, 2014). For example, women enter college as STEM undergraduates at an equal rate as men but drop out of post-doctorate and academic positions at a very high rate, and as a result, only about 25% of fulltime STEM faculty are female (Hyde et al., 2014). Women may be underrepresented in the STEM workforce because sexual harassment leads them to change occupations.

Outside of STEM, the rate of sexual harassment is especially high in several traditionally male-dominated domains in which females are the numerical minority. For example, 69% of women in military samples reported experiencing sexually harassing behavior, compared to 58% of women in the academic sector, 46% in the private sector, and 43% in the government sector (Ilies et al., 2003). Indicating further evidence of male resistance to female leadership, the risk of sexual harassment greatly increases for women in the workplace when they have attained higher education, are in supervisory positions, or work in an occupation that falls in a traditionally masculine domain (Eagly and Carli, 2007). Additionally, women who trespass traditional gender norms in terms of occupation and behavior are more likely to be sexually harassed and socially undermined by men (Berdahl et al., 2010). The increased prevalence of harassment in male-dominated domains and among agentic women who violate feminine gender norms may signify male resentment and a form of retaliation to competent women succeeding in traditionally masculine settings (Carli, 2004; Eagly & Carli, 2007; Leskinen, Cortina, & Kabat, 2011).

Chapter 1: Sexual Harassment in STEM

Women today are more widely represented across work domains and more active in the workforce than ever before. They represent about 57.1% of the total U.S. labor force, including about 51.5% of all workers in high-paying management, professional, and related occupations (U.S. Bureau of Labor Statistics, 2013; Toossi, 2012). For the first time in U.S. history, women are not only surpassing men in employment rates, but they also comprise a majority of the students seeking college degrees. Although women now comprise about half of the total U.S. labor force, women's advancement in STEM related fields is still filled with obstacles. Perhaps the most pervasive, detrimental, and harmful obstacle obstructing the advancement of women in STEM fields is the occurrence of sexual harassment in the workplace.

A 2009 survey completed by current employees found 31% of females and 7% of males reported they have been sexually harassed at work (Kowalewsk et al., 2009). Women entering into Science, Technology, Engineering, and Math related fields are not only vastly outnumbered by men, they are also subjected to an extremely high rate of sexual harassment. One survey of over 600 female scientists, found that nearly two thirds experienced some form of sexual harassment (Hyde, Nelson, College, and Rutherford, 2014). Thus, current survey evidence indicates

4

that women in STEM are more than twice as likely to experience sexual harassment at work than women employed in non-STEM fields. Women in STEM may also be at higher risk for physical harassment in addition to unwanted verbal comments. Nearly 20% of female scientists reported that they experienced sexual assault or unwanted physical sexual contact (Hyde, Nelson, College, and Rutherford, 2014). Thus, females in STEM experience a difficult, potentially dangerous, work environment that may discourage women from entering into science and math related fields (Zadronzy, 2014).

Most female victims of sexual harassment in STEM are subordinates who work under their perpetrators, with 96% of females reporting that they were trainees or employees at the time the harassment took place (Hyde, Nelson, College, and Rutherford, 2014). The negative psychological and job related impacts that often result from being harassed by a supervisor could be one possible reason why so few women persist in STEM fields (Hyde, Nelson, College, and Rutherford, 2014). For example, women enter college as undergraduates at an equal rate as men but drop out of post-doctorate and academic positions at a very high rate and as a result only about 25% of fulltime STEM faculty are female (Hyde, Nelson, College, and Rutherford, 2014). A sexually harassing work environment may partially explain why so many women choose to leave STEM during the first years of their working careers. Younger female STEM employees just entering the workforce reported the highest rates of sexual harassment among all STEM employees (Zadrozny, 2014). As a result, female junior staffs in STEM are at a high risk of experiencing unwanted sexual encounters that may interfere with their training on the job, work performance, and job satisfaction.

Although there is an abundance of previous research that has indicated the presence of gender bias in multiple domains, very few studies have examined gender biases among STEM faculty that could contribute to the discrimination of females and minority members seeking to advance in academic settings (Moss-Racusin et al., 2012). Relating to gender bias, Moss-Racusin et al. 2012, found evidence that male and female STEM faculty members in multiple departments hold subtle gender biases that favor male students. That is, science faculty evaluated male lab manager applicants as more competent, more hirable, and reported they should be offered higher starting salaries than female applicants with identical qualifications (Moss-Racusin et al., 2012). Thus, there seems to be evidence that indicates a possible presence of discrimination of females in STEM projected by STEM faculty members who reported fewer positive responses (level of competence, likelihood of being hired, and starting salary) for female applicants in relation to male applicants applying for the same position, despite the presence of identical job qualifications between the groups (Moss-Racusin et al., 2012). Interestingly, perceptions of competence have been found to mediate the relationship between applicant gender and hireability, indicating that because males are perceived to be more competent, they are hired more often than females (Moss-Racusin et al., 2012). To summarize, the female target group has been denied equal treatment in the evaluation process due to stereotypes of males being higher in competence and lower in warmth than female applicants, especially relating to science and math (Fiske, Cuddy, Glick, & Xu, 2002).

Chapter 2: Online Forms of Sexual Harassment

Along with the advent of the internet and other technological advances in the workplace, employee sexual harassment is increasingly occurring online (Boyd, 2010). A Pew Research Center's American Trends Panel (2014) that surveyed 2,849 web users measuring the prevalence of all types of online harassment reported by U.S. adults found that 25% of adult females experienced some form of sexual harassment online, and 24% of all adults witnessed someone being sexually harassed online for a prolonged period of time (Pew Research Center, 2014). Such a high prevalence of sexual harassment reported by targets and witnessed by outsiders underlies the importance for future research examining causes and antecedents of online sexual harassment in order to provide organizations with empirical evidence to guide the development of effective policy that prevent such behaviors from taking place.

Online harassment may be particularly prevalent in technology fields and other highly masculine domains where women are the numerical minority. However, the influence of organizational norms should also be considered in future research when measuring perceptions of online sexual harassment because they have been shown to be related to the perpetrators' decisions to commit sexually offensive acts and the targets' reaction to experiencing the behavior (Keyton, Ferguson, & Rhodes, 2001; Espinoza & Cunningham, 2010; Berdahl & Raver, 2012). Lastly, despite the abundance of existing research that examines perceptions of face-to-face incidents of sexual harassment, there has been an increasing need in recent years for researchers to examine reactions to online behaviors that may be perceived as sexual harassment (Berkley & Kaplan, 2009; Boyd, 2010). Future research will likely increasingly measure perceptions of such behaviors.

Chapter 3: Perceptions of Sexual Harassment

Sexual harassment continues to receive a tremendous amount of attention in research and is extremely important in ultimately determining if sexually harassing behaviors are acceptable in the workplace and the likelihood that incidents of sexual harassment are reported to organizations. Individuals have become increasingly concerned with the possibility of sexual abuse in several public institutions, particularly the workforce. Sexual harassment's effect on the workplace has become increasingly bothersome because it is expected and intended to be a safe environment for obtaining knowledge (Mohipp & Senn, 2008). Additionally, reported cases of sexual harassment in the STEM fields are exceptionally high, with over two thirds of female scientists reporting unwelcomed sexual behavior in the past five years (Zadronzy, 2014). As a result, sexual harassment of female scientists has received increasing attention from researchers in recent years (Fitzgerald, 1991; Zadronzy, 2014).

Surprisingly, sexual harassment has many aspects that remain unstudied. A surprisingly miniscule amount of research has been completed on sexual harassment outside of reviewing reports from victims (Barting & Eisenman, 1993). Perceptions of what constitutes sexual harassment are an extremely important factor in determining if any individual case is reported. Further, understanding perceptions of sexual harassment should increase the understanding of what is considered socially acceptable and unacceptable in an academic setting. The two most significant ways research has found employee perceptions of sexual harassment are by the gender of the observer and the perpetrator's power in relation to the target.

Chapter 4: Gender Differences in Sexual Harassment Perceptions

Men and women tend to have different perceptions of sexual harassment. Mohipp and Sinn (2008) found that male participants scored perpetrators less accountable and held the victims more responsible than the female participants. Similarly, Bartling and Eisenman (1993) found that women in their study reported sexually threatening situations in more scenarios than did men, and as a result also reported higher levels of harassment. Bursik's (1992) findings indicated that women reported the male perpetrator's actions as offensive or inappropriate more often than men. Similarly, females were more likely to report the behavior they marked offensive or inappropriate as sexual harassment than were men. Marks and Nelson (1993) also found higher perceptions of sexual harassment in women compared to men, in which females evaluated all four scenarios of potential sexual harassment as more inappropriate than the male participants in the study.

Bartling and Eisenman (1993) gathered a sample of male and female college students who completed a sexual harassment proclivities scale in order to compare gender differences in perception of sexual harassment. Their scores were then compared on several different measures including sex role stereotyping, rape myth acceptance, and sexual exploitation. The majority of the findings indicated statistically significant results for both males and females, with males generally displaying higher rates of endorsing sexually inappropriate behavior as acceptable. The study also found that both men and women displaying adverbial sexual beliefs and weak empathy skills were more likely to initiate sexually harassing behaviors than those who did not (Bartling & Eisenman, 1993). However, women in the study scored higher in sexually threatening situations than did men, and as a result were more likely to report the behavior as sexual harassment (Bartling & Eisenman, 1993).

In a similar study by Marks and Nelson (1993), researchers measured the effects of gender on sexual harassing behaviors. A sample of undergraduate students viewed and evaluated one of four videotaped vignettes that showed potentially sexually inappropriate behaviors by male and female professors to students of the opposite sex. Overall, the male students in the study ranked the professor's behavior as less harassing than the females in the study. Their results remain consistent with other data of sexual harassment that show females are more likely to label a particular behavior as sexual harassment than males. For example, a 2014 survey that polled over 1,500 Canadians who are currently working or have worked outside the home found that 34% of men and only 21% of women found it acceptable to call a colleague's outfit "sexy" and 34% of men and just 16% of women believe that the issue of workplace sexual harassment is "overblown" (Angus Reid, 2014).

Chapter 5: Perpetrator Power and Differences in Sexual Harassment Perceptions

Previous studies have indicated that the behavior of alleged perpetrators in positions of power are more often labeled as sexually inappropriate than those with little or no formal organizational authority over the target. For example, Fitzgerald (1991) found that the power level of the initiator (position of formal or direct authority) affected the degree to which any interaction was viewed as harassment. Similarly, Mohipp and Senn (2008) discovered that perceptions of harassment were directly related to the perpetrator's position of power over the victim. For example, a professor's behavior towards students was more likely viewed as sexual harassment than in the scenarios in which student harassed the professor (Mohipp & Senn, 2008).

Bursik (1992) completed a study measuring gender, gender role, and the power position of the harasser on perceptions of harassment by having a sample of 124 individuals evaluate several vignettes displaying different situations of potential sexual harassment. The results indicated that the vignettes involving a perpetrator with perceived power were more likely to be viewed as sexual harassment than those without a person of power. In addition, male perpetrators were given higher ratings of sexual harassment than were their female counterparts.

Further, males in the study ranked the male perpetrators in a more positive light than females. Overall, women evaluated the males' behavior as much less appropriate in the context of the interaction.

Fitzgerald (1991) measured perceptions of sexual harassment based on gender in academic settings by randomly assigning faculty members and graduate students to review five types of sexual harassment. The five types of sexual harassment measured were gender harassment, seductive behavior, sexual bribery, sexual coercion, and sexual imposition. Participants were each assigned a scenario that displayed the harassed student as either a graduate or undergraduate. In addition, half of the scenarios portrayed the professor having direct power over the student, while the other half portrayed no power connection at all. The results indicated that neither the grade level of the victim nor the degree of the faculty member's power over the victim influenced the ratings of the situations. However, the study did find that women were more likely than men to view explicatory coercive scenarios as sexual harassment.

Mohipp and Senn (2008) completed a study comparing graduate students' perceptions of sexual harassment scenarios with and without contra power situations. Participants were asked to rank different sexual harassment scenarios with a male perpetrator and a female victim. The independent variable, type of harassment, was manipulated by making half of the harassment scenarios have the instructor as the perpetrator, and half of the scenarios showing a student perpetrator harass a professor. The results indicated that the participants rated contra power sexual harassment less severely than the traditional sexual harassment cases. Regardless of teaching experience, women ranked both types of harassment scenarios more negative than men.

Azy, Pitterman, and Yitzhaki (1995) tested whether reports of sexual harassment involving male perpetrators with positions of power were more common than men who did not have power over the female victim. In addition, the study tested whether power differentials between men and women at work and in educational settings produce different perceptions of sexual harassment by comparing incident reports of two samples of women. One sample consisted of urban women exposed to a more Western style society and work place. The second sample consisted of women living and working in a more secluded, egalitarian society. Women in both groups were matched by variables including type of employment, age, and education level. The findings revealed that overall rates of sexual harassment cases and reactions to sexual harassment incidents were nearly identical between the two groups. In addition, male perpetrators with positions of power over female victims were not any more prevalent than males with no power in either of the groups. It appears, fairly or unfairly, supervisors are held to a higher standard regarding sexual harassment than employees. Specifically, those in positions of power are more likely to have a complaint filed against them through the Equal Employment Opportunity Commission (EEOC) than employees for the same type of behavior.

Interestingly, although the scores of sexual harassment for men in power tend to be higher than those who are not, previous studies refute this assumption from being true in reality. Azy et. al. (1995) found that there was not a significant difference between women who are sexually harassed by supervisors and those who were harassed by coworkers. Contrary to public opinion, it seems power differential does not lead to abuse of the organizational position or to exercising mastery or control over women, per se. This finding is significant for employers to keep in mind as it indicates that supervisors are no more likely to perpetrate sexual harassment onto subordinates than co-workers are with fellow co-workers.

There are some notable limitations to existing studies that could limit findings to the general public. First, many samples consisted of undergraduate college students, which limit the experiment's external validity to other populations. In addition, there were a disproportionately high number of females in some of the studies. For example, in one study since over two thirds of the participants in the study were women, the overall ratings could be skewed towards female conceptions of sexual harassment. As a result, employers should interpret these effects with caution, as employees may likely be less sensitive to actual incidents of sexual harassment than students. Since perpetrator status was found to be a significant factor in ratings of sexual harassment, it seems plausible that additional research should be completed on the subject. More specifically, the general belief that men with power over females are more likely to sexually harass their subordinates than other males should be tested. In addition, research comparing the similarities of failed sexual harassment cases against male superiors could be used to help distinguish which reports can be labeled as legitimate cases of sexual harassment in the future. Research on this issue has led to the general conclusion that males in positions of power are more likely to be perceived as using sexually inappropriate behavior than males without power in a sexual harassment situation.

To conclude, previous research on sexual harassment has shown that those with inherit positions of power over victims are more likely to be perceived as being sexually inappropriate than individuals who do not have inherit power over victims. Additionally, prior research has indicated that women tend to be more sensitive to sexual harassment than men.

Chapter 6: Employer Liability for Sexual Harassment

According to the EEOC 1990 Enforcement Guidance on Current Issues of Sexual Harassment, it is unlawful for an employer to "fail or refuse to hire or to discharge any individual, or otherwise to discriminate against any individual with respect to his compensation, terms conditions or privileges of employment, because of such individual's race, color, religion, sex, or national origin." In 1980 the EEOC declared sexual harassment, or any unwelcome behavior of a sexual nature in the workplace, a violation of the 1964 Civil Rights Act, Title VII, Section 703. Many employers have to contend with a fair share of sexual harassment in the workplace, which can often go unreported. Recent survey research suggests that anywhere between 35-70% of women and 10-20% of men have experienced some form of sexual harassment at work, although only 32% of women and only 7% of men reported experiencing sexual harassment at work (Kowalewsk et al., 2009; Zadronzy, 2014).

Additionally, employers may be lacking programs to address such behavior. A recent study found that only 62% of companies offer some sort of sexual harassment training program, while 97% reported they have a written sexual harassment policy (Society for Human Management, 1999). Training programs have been found to prevent sexual harassment and may prove to be beneficial in the long term, outside of potential court cases and settlements that often involve punitive compensation, there is a current lack of knowledge, resources, and finances present in many companies.

Chapter 7: Legal Definition and Types of Sexual Harassment

While the legal definition of sexual harassment depends on the jurisdiction, most model the definition outlined in Title VII of the Civil Rights Act. All employers with 15 or more employees are required by law to adhere to Title VII policies (employers with fewer than 15 employees are governed by state law). According to the guidelines outlined in Title VII by the EEOC, any unwelcome sexual advances, requests for sexual favors, and other verbal or physical conduct of a sexual nature constitute sexual harassment when one of two conditions are met: (1) submission to or rejection of such conduct by an individual is used as the basis for employment decisions affecting such individuals, or (2) the unwelcome conduct unreasonably interferes with an individual's work performance or creates an intimidating, hostile, or abusive work environment (EEOC, 1980; 29 C.F.R. § 1604.11 [1980]).

According to Title VII of the 1964 Civil Rights Act, the two types of sexual harassment that occur at work are "Quid Pro Quo" harassment and "Hostile Work Environment" harassment. Importantly, according to the 1990 EEOC Enforcement Guidance, the Supreme Courts in Vinson established that both types of sexual harassment are actionable under the 1964 Civil Rights Act, Title VII,

Section 703 as forms of sexual discrimination in the workplace. While Quid Pro Quo harassment refers to implied or explicit offers of sexual behavior in exchange for some tangible workplace (e.g. promotion, raise) or to avoid a detriment (e.g. demotion), Hostile Work Environment harassment refers to sexually inappropriate conduct that is so severe and pervasive that it interferes with an individual's ability to perform their job or creates an intimidating or hostile work environment (EEOC, 2014). If either Quid Pro Quo or Hostile Work Environment harassment can be proven in businesses with 15 or more employees, the employer may be liable for compensatory (e.g. monetary loss, pain, and suffering) and punitive damages for allowing such behavior to occur (Thomas Reuters, 2014). Liability for either type of harassment depends on what steps the employer took to prevent sexual harassment, whether or not the employer promptly took action to obstruct the inappropriate behavior after they were made aware, and a formal complaint describing the conduct was filed with the EEOC within 45 days of the occurrence (Thomson Reuters, 2014). Thus, swift and decisive actions should be taken by the organization to investigate potential harassment and ensure that such incidents do not continue by issuing appropriate sanctions to the perpetrator if they are found guilty.

Chapter 8: Quid Pro Quo vs. Hostile Environment Harassment

Quid Pro Quo, Latin for "this for that," harassment refers to a trade of certain sexual actions for favorable treatment at work. Quid Pro Quo is not very common among sexual harassment cases and is typically committed by an employer or supervisor over a subordinate and usually involves some sort of economic injury to the target (RAIIN, 2014). Conversely, Hostile Work Environment sexual harassment refers to persistent and severe unwanted conduct of a sexual nature (e.g. persistent or severe jokes, lewd postures, leering) that creates a threatening/hostile work environment or leads to detrimental employment decisions of the target (e.g. the target choose to quit their job because of a threatening work environment). Hostile Work Environment harassment cases are filed frequently and constitute up to 95% of sexual harassment cases and are commonly committed by employers, co-workers, and non-employees who make up the "work environment" (RAIIN, 2014). According to the EEOC, an act is more likely to meet the standards of Hostile Work Environment harassment and be grounds for legal action if the conduct was physical, rather than just verbal, the conduct occurred with high frequency, the act was blatantly offensive, the alleged harasser was a supervisor as opposed to a co-worker, others joined in perpetrating the harassment, the harassment singled out the victim instead of being targeted as several individuals, the target subjectively believed the conduct was hostile/offensive, and a reasonable person in the target's position would objectively believe the conduct was hostile/offensive.

Importantly, although Quid Pro Quo and Hostile Environment harassments are distinct claims, the two often occur together, since there is often overlap (EEOC, 2010). For example, an employee's tangible job conditions are affected when a sexually Hostile Work Environment results in their constructive discharge (EEOC, 2010). Similarly, a supervisor who makes implicit threats from a Hostile Work Environment may be charged with both types of sexual harassment. Claims of "hostile environment" also commonly result in claims of constructive discharge, meaning the hostile environment leads the target employee to quit their job. If "hostile environment" claims are proven, employers are held responsible for employee constructive discharge when they impose intolerable working conditions that would reasonably compel an employee to quit, regardless if the employer intended to force the target to quit their job (EEOC, 2010).

In addition, employers who take retaliation against victims' accusations of sexual harassment have violated Title VII in a different way. Retaliation to sexual harassment claims are distinct from the alleged sexual harassment itself, and as a result have separate, yet specific legal disciplinary protocol that can be used against perpetrators. According to the EEOC, sexual harassment often culminates in a retaliatory discharge if a victim tells the harasser or their employer they will no longer submit to the harassment; in this case, both sexual harassment and retaliation are in violation of Section 704(a) of Title VII making the employer more liable to financial sanctions (EEOC, 2010).

Chapter 9: Practical Implications for Employers

According to the EEOC, sexual acts must be unwelcome to be considered sexual harassment, making most welcome sexual or romantic interactions between two consenting people at work legal (though they may still violate company policy). However, in order to determine if a particular act was welcomed, courts will individually review the circumstances of each sexual harassment case and often rule that a victim does not need to explicitly say or do anything to indicate that the act was unwelcome. For example, acts are often deemed unwelcomed by courts if the alleged harasser has a position of power over the target, if the target could fear punishment of being fired for protesting, the alleged harasser is physically threatening, or if the target ends a previously consenting relationship with the harasser (EEOC, 2014). Thus, certain sexual acts may constitute as harassment regardless of the expressed intent of the perpetrator. For example, American politician and former U.S. Representative Anthony Weiner resigned from Congress in June 2011 due to a sexting scandal involving him sending a nude picture of his genitals to 6 different women online. Although Weiner claims the online exchanges with the women were consensual, some of the women claim that the pictures were sent without their consent or approval (Williams, 2011). Weiner also claimed that the tweeted photos he sent to a female reporter were part of a joke, however the reporter claimed the pictures

Wiener sent of his erection were unasked for, which may likely constitute harassment (Williams, 2011). If the female reporter's claim that the pictures were not welcomed or encouraged are true, Wiener's behavior was, in the very least, an act of sexual aggression. Many argue that this act alone was enough to lead him to resign and formally end his political career because it was unwelcomed by the target.

All unwelcome workplace conduct on or off duty may be sexual or nonsexual and must be reviewed in the context, however, laws generally do not prohibit minor isolated incidents of unwelcome conduct (e.g. such as teasing) unless it is so severe or frequent that it can be classified as a Hostile Work Environment (EEOC, 2014). For example, hugging, grabbing, staring, sexual pranks, sexual teasing, blocking victim's path, and written/oral requests or statements may be considered sexual or nonsexual depending on context (US Department of State Sexual Harassment Policy, 2014). Despite this, it is likely more practical and beneficial for employers to assume that explicit consent does not guarantee protection under the law. As previously mentioned, if the conduct is physical, involves someone in a position of power, or occurs frequently, it is probably best for employers to deal with the case as quickly as possible, and adopt company policies when needed.

Chapter 10: Organizational Changes and Policy Recommendations for Employers

If a complaint is filed to the appropriate federal agency within 45 days of the alleged sexual harassment and the investigation conducted by the EEOC concludes no settlement between the target and the employer, victims of sexual harassing behavior can choose to file a Title XII law suit (Thomson Reuters, 2014). The organization is liable if they knew about or should have known about the alleged sexually harassing behavior(s) unless they took immediate corrective action once informed (Thomson Reuters, 2014). The target has the option of not reporting the sexual harassment directly to their supervisor, and instead directly filing a complaint to the EEOC. However, if the target does not report the incident or fails to allow their employer a chance to address the sexually harassing behavior using company procedures and policies, the target may likely lose in court (Thomson Reuters, 2014). Thus, it is in the target's best interest to file an official complaint to their employer or HR Department before filing a complaint with EEOC whenever possible. Implementing a company policy that encourages victims of sexual harassment in the workplace to report such behavior while ensuring that their identities will be protected may likely result in more frequently reported behavior of sexual harassment that can be solved "in house" by company policies which would likely improve the workplace environment and lead to fewer

EEOC cases and law suits that normally would have been filed without informing the employer.

Employers can not underestimate the importance of having established, time-efficient company procedures for dealing with sexual harassment complaints before they are filed with the EEOC. If company procedures do not apply to a particular complaint, employers should immediately take corrective action to stop the occurrence of the alleged sexual harassment and provide documentation that they attempted to resolve the matter in a timely fashion. Providing evidence or documentation proving the employer immediately followed company protocol after they were made aware of the occurrence of sexual harassment is often used to determine if the employer is liable for the behavior or not. Convoluted or rigid sexual harassment policies, especially those democratic in nature, may want to be adjusted at the discretion of the employer in order to provide the best solution for each case as quickly and as efficiently as possible. For example, an open-door policy that involves the organization and target coming to a mutual agreement for future action may increase the chances the intervention is effective and satisfies the target as much as possible while maintaining confidentiality during the investigation.

Chapter 11: Causes of Gender Discrimination in the Workplace

Previous studies provide support to the idea of complimentary stereotypes, in which members of high and low-status groups are perceived to have offsetting strengths and weaknesses (Jost et al., 2004). Exposure to such offsetting commentary stereotypes such as "impoverished yet happy" and "wealthy yet unhappy" has been shown to increase endorsements of system justification efforts (Kay & Jost, 2003). Proponents of System Justification Theory (SJT) argue that such complimentary stereotypes ensure the persistence of outgroup favoritism and bias against target group members by encouraging system justification motives prompted through the belief that high and low-status groups have offsetting strengths, and that no group in society is without positive and negative values (Jost et al., 2004). Similarly, the presence of complimentary gender stereotypes in which women are thought of as being highly communal and warm but not agentic, has been shown to increase endorsement of system justifying statements that support unjustified gender biases that exist in the status quo (Kay & Jost, 2003; Dovidio, 2010). It seems plausible that complimentary gender stereotypes that view women as more communal and less agentic may have influenced the gender bias found among STEM faculty members that favored male profiles as more competent and less warm than female profiles. Inflated ratings of competence of male profiles likely led to higher ratings of hireability and starting salary found among men (Moss-Racusin et al., 2012). Nevertheless, there seems to be some evidence that complimentary gender stereotypes that justify the systematic mistreatment of women may be unconsciously implanted by faculty in STEM and could very well contribute to the lack of female representation in science and math fields.

Chapter 12: Positive Stereotypes

Positive stereotypes make sweeping generalizations that Asians are exceptionally skillful in math and science, ambitiously seek careers in math or science related fields, and highly value academic success (Siy & Cheryan, 2013). However, research has indicated that the use of positive stereotypes during evaluative processes can lead to several aversive effects, in that they depersonalize the target's unique set of skills and personality characteristics, are often found to be offensive, and may bias results at the expense of individuals to which the stereotype is not directed (Trytten, 2012; Siy & Cheryan, 2013). Positive and negative stereotypes about different target groups make sweeping generalizations about individuals based on assumptions that may be false. For example, despite the prevalence of positive stereotypes ascribed to Asian Americans, research has shown that the academic record of Asians is not significantly different from any other racial group and that Asian American students do not academically conform to such positive-stereotypes (Trytten et al., 2012). Despite this, many Asian Americans report that they are frequently assumed to be hardworking, skilled in math, uncomplaining, intelligent, and seeking educational prestige by their peers (Trytten et al., 2012; Siy & Cheryan, 2013). Consequently, connotations from the negative stereotypes associated with African Americans, Hispanics, and females as having low math and science ability, limited career aspirations, and low work ethic may attenuate ratings of competence and hireability, while positive stereotypes that associate minority members and females with being friendly may simultaneously inflate perceptions of warmth to offset the diminished perceived competence (Dovidio, 2010; Siy & Cheryan, 2013). Taken altogether, these stereotypes fuel the acceptance of uncivil behaviors toward women in the STEM fields.

Chapter 13: System Justification

System Justification Theory (SJT) argues that people want to hold favorable attitudes about themselves and about their own groups, but they also want to hold favorable attitudes about social systems of society that affect their status (Jost et al., 2004). The theory holds that along with ego and group motives, there is also an underlining motive to protect the existing social order by viewing it as fair. Perhaps most significant, is that system justification motives are sometimes capable of overriding ego and group justification motives associated with the protection of individual and collective interests and esteem (Jost et al., 2004). This finding explains why members of disadvantaged or target groups sometimes support and internalize harmful stereotypes about their own group even more than members of the dominant groups in power. SJT can help explain the current gender gap in STEM fields by assuming that females have internalized the system justifying belief that males are more competent in math and science and therefore women are less likely to pursue higher education and careers in STEM fields. If STEM faculty members have also internalized this belief, SJT would shed light on the gender bias found during the STEM hiring process by revealing internalized support for gender stereotypes that favor males as more competent in science and math than females. More significantly, SJT sheds light on the perplexing finding that female faculty members expressed just as much gender bias against female applicants as the male faculty members. Similarly, any racial bias found during the STEM hiring process could also be explained by SJT in that STEM faculty members could be implicitly justifying the current lack of representation of racial minority members in math and science related fields by endorsing long-standing racial stereotypes that views underrepresented minority members as less competent in science and math (Sniderman and Piazza, 1993).

SJT also alleges that the general ideological motive to justify the existing social order is often the strongest among target groups who are most harmed by the system (Jost et al., 2004). Specifically, SJT asserts that system justifying motives operate unconsciously; it helps explain why members of target groups would endorse their subordination (Brescoll et al., 2013). For example, one study found that African American respondents generally accepted unfavorable stereotypes of their own group as lazy, irresponsible, and violent to a greater extent than the European American respondents did (Sniderman and Piazza, 1993). Similarly, SJT can be applied to help explain the perplexing gender-bias that existed among female STEM faculty members who rated male applicants as more competent and hirable than female applicants with identical credentials (Moss-Racusin et al., 2012).

According to SJT, female faculty members have internalized the "males are naturally more competent at science and math than females" stereotype and use it to favor males in order to justify the current gender parity that exists in the STEM fields. The need to justify the existing social order in STEM trumped female faculty members' expression of group favoritism that would have protected their own gender's interests, and resulted in outgroup favoritism marked by an evaluative preference for male applicants (Jost et al., 2002). This is consistent with previous studies that have shown that members of vulnerable populations often hold more favorable attitudes toward members of more advantaged groups (Jost et al., 2000; Beasley & Fischer, 2012; Brescoll et al., 2013). The need to justify the social order is so strong, it trumps the protection of other women's interests, even though STEM faculty are likely aware that they are already vastly underrepresented in STEM fields. Ultimately, SJT contends that there is a cycle of underrepresentation of women and minority members in STEM that is sustained by internalized gender and racial biases which arise from stereotypes used to justify the existing inequality that exists in science and math.

Chapter 14: Essentialist Explanations

Another reason why so few female and minority racial members have persisted in the STEM fields of higher education may be due to system justifying motives that endorse essentialist explanations that explain group differences as immutable (Brescoll et al., 2013). That is, if members of disadvantaged groups accept the notion of immutable biological differences, they are more likely to protect the existing system by endorsing long-standing stereotypes that emphasize innate biological gender and racial differences in certain subjects because such differences are incapable of being changed (Brescoll et al., 2013). Specifically, the current underrepresentation of women and minority members in STEM can be partly explained by implicit system justifying motives that endorse essentialist racial and gender differences in math and science ability that are both innate and immutable (Jost et al., 2004; Brescoll et al., 2013). For example, if individuals of target groups agree with the system justifying essentialist statements, e.g., "the reason why there are more male science professors than female science professors is mainly attributable to immutable innate differences between the genders," they are likely to view the system as stable and unchangeable over time and are more likely to accept the current social order (Keller, 2005; Brescoll et al., 2013).

Essentialist beliefs explain the current underrepresentation of racial minority members and females in STEM through the endorsement of essentialist stereotypes that categorize women and minority members as having lower innate competence in math and science than males, which justifies the current inequality in STEM fields (Fiske, Cuddy, Glick, & Xu, 2002). Essentialist beliefs account for the gender and racial imparity in STEM by implying innate differences that are immutable, e.g. women are naturally more nurturing and warm than men, but less competent, and SJT theory contends that there is an underlining motive for females and minority members to endorse such beliefs that view them as less competent in science and math than males and that the underrepresentation that has persisted in STEM is unchangeable (Keller, 2005; Brescoll et al., 2013).

Scientists in many different fields have long debated whether and to what extent group differences are based on essential biological factors. Brescoll, Newman, & Uhlmann (2013) found that when the dominant existing system is under threat, both men and women have a higher tendency to endorse essentialists explanation for gender differences that attribute innate and immutable differences in biology for the disproportionate number of women entering science and math fields. If gender differences are described as immutable or unchangeable, men and women are both more likely to use essentialist explanations to justify inequalities between them if the social system is threatened (Brescoll, Newman, & Uhlmann. 2013). System affirmations caused less endorsement of essential ideologies that attribute differences to fixed genetic factors, whereas system threats increased essential ideological endorsements (Brescoll, Newman, & Uhlmann. 2013). Resultantly, it seems that a threat to the dominant social system creates an unconscious motive for members of that society to support essential ideologies to support the current inequalities in the social hierarchy if the inequalities are perceived to be immutable. However, if current differences and inequalities between groups are perceived to be changeable, then individuals would be less likely to endorse essentialist beliefs. As a result, it seems practical to emphasize the importance of the mutability of the current inequalities in society by showing that they can be changed.

Summary

Discrimination of women in the workforce and the prevalence of sexual harassment have diminished greatly since Title VII of the Civil Rights Act was passed in 1964, with employers being held more accountable for their workplace environment than ever before. In order to provide a non-threatening work environment and to avoid litigation claims of alleged harassment, more and more employers are implementing organizational policies and procedures for addressing instances of sexual harassment promptly and fairly. However, with the ever increasing amount of sexual harassment complaints made annually to the EEOC, it is vital that organizations take a preventive approach to such complaints by informing their employees of acceptable and unacceptable work behavior and training all employees to uphold and be responsible for following a firm organizational harassment policy to prevent such harassment from occurring in the first place. Further, certain male-dominated workplaces, particularly in the STEM fields, should take particular precautions to ensure all employees do not create a hostile or threatening work environment for women. It may be particularly important to ensure supervisors in STEM fields are aware and adhere to their organizational harassment policies in order to prevent female subordinates from being subjected to offensive sexual conduct. Additionally, in order to reduce unwanted sexual behavior, it is vital that the work culture does not

41

adhere to long-standing gendered stereotypes about females that justify the mistreatment and harassment of women. Creating a more supportive work culture that is free of gender base stereotypes, and lowering instances of sexual harassment through the implementation of an effective organization policy, may increase the number of women who enter and persist in traditionally male-dominated fields.

My hope is that this book makes it easier for employers to understand the causes of a sexually harassing work environment, the bottom line consequences associated with maintaining an organization that is tolerant of gender discriminating behaviors, and policy implementation strategies that have empirically been proven to reduce the prevalence of sexually harassing behaviors at work and increase the likelihood that such behaviors are reported. I believe the ultimate decision to provide a supportive, equal opportunity work environment that is free from gender discrimination will ultimately prove to be a win-win for employers and employees in STEM fields by improving previously hindered career aspirations of individual female employees while simultaneously increasing organizational bottom line revenue by reducing turnover, increasing organizational commitment, and improving the motivation of high performing female employees.

Supporting Materials

Examples of Quid Pro Quo Sexual Harassment in the Workplace

- *Employer tells employee more likely to get promotion if dresses sexier (Perpetrator guilty regardless if employee submits or agrees to sexual act).*
- *A salary increase is offered based on the contingency of sexual intercourse.*
- *The rejection of sexual advances leads a supervisor to deny tangible salary benefits to a female employee he asked out on a date.*
- *A direct or implied threat of retaliation if a target does not agree to a sexual request (May be committed by Employer/Supervisor or co-worker).*
- *Any sexual request that is unwelcomed by an employee and involves any aspect relating to job .*

List 1. Examples of Quid Pro Quo Sexual Harassment in the Workplace. Inspired by the Advocates for Human Right's Stop Violence Against Women Project.

Retrieved from: http://www.stopvaw.org/quid_pro_quo_sexual_harassment.

Examples of Hostile Environment Sexual Harassment in the Workplace

- *Offensive or teasing statements about women that are frequent/disturbing enough to create a hostile work environment.*
- *Sexually suggestive statements or jokes that cause an employee to make an aversive employment decision.*
- *Invasive questions about one's private life or personal appearance (e.g. that dress looks very sexy on you, where did you get it?).*
- *Inappropriate staring or prolonged gazing at eyes or other body parts.*
- *Unwelcomed touching, hugging, or kissing (even if playful).*
- *Other types of inappropriate physical contact.*
- *Inappropriate or sexual emails or text messages.*
- *Unwelcomed invitations to go out (especially if repeated).*
- *Sexually explicit pictures or gifts.*
- *Sexual gestures or unwelcomed exposure of body.*
- *Requests for sexual acts.*
- *Repeated inappropriate advances on email or social networking websites.*

List 2. Examples of Hostile Environment Sexual Harassment in the Workplace. Modified from the Australian Human Rights Commission.

Retrieved from: https://www.humanrights.gov.au/chapter-5-working-without-fear-results-sexual-harassment-national-telephone-survey-2012).

Questions Commonly Asked in Court to Determine if Behavior Constitutes as Sexual Harassment

- *Would a reasonable victim of the same sex as the plaintiff consider the comments/gestures severe or pervasive enough to constitute a hostile working environment? ("Reasonable woman or man standard"- Used to determine Perception/Intent in court.)*
- *How often did the behavior occur?*
- *What was the nature of the behavior? Was conduct physical or verbal?*
- *Has this behavior been exhibited to other employees?*
- *Was the act/statement patently offensive or threatening?*
- *Is the alleged harasser a supervisor of the target?*
- *Did others at work join in perpetrating the harassment or was it just one individual?*
- *Did the harassment single out one victim or was it targeted at many individuals?*
- *Did the target subjectively find the conduct as hostile or offensive?*
- *Did the employer promptly take corrective actions to obstruct the continuance of such behavior if they were made aware of its presence?*

List 3. Considerations commonly considered in court to determine liability of sexual harassment cases. Modified from the Human Right's Stop Violence Against Women Project.

Retrieved from: http://www.stopvaw.org/quid_pro_quo_sexual_harassment.

EEOC Recommendations for Employers

- *Train all HR managers and all employees on EEOC laws and their employment rights.*
- *Vigorously follow and enforce sexual harassment policy after it is implemented.*
- *Provide clear explanation of prohibited behavior.*
- *Provide specific examples of prohibited behavior.*
- *Ensure employees that make complaints will be protected from retaliation of the organization or their supervisor(s).*
- *Include clearly described complaint process with example.*
- *Give assurance that the employer will protect the confidentiality of harassment complaints as much as possible.*
- *Include a statement saying that the complaint process provides a prompt, complete, and impartial investigation.*
- *Assurance that the employer will take immediate, appropriate, and corrective action when it determines if sexual harassment has occurred.*
- *Closely adhere to policy guidelines.*

List 4. EEOC suggested information for employers to include in sexual harassment policy to avoid legal liability and maximize help to employee targets of sexual harassment.

Retrieved from: http://www.eeoc.gov/eeoc/initiatives/e-race/bestpractices-employers.cfm

EEOC Questions Considered for Non-physical Sexual Harassment Claims

- *Did the Harasser(s) single out the charging party?*
- *Did the charging party choose to participate?*
- *What was the relationship between the charging party and the alleged harasser(s)?*
- *Were the remarks hostile or derogatory?*
- *Has an employee forfeited their right to work in an environment free from sexual harassment by choice?*

List 5. Equal Employment Opportunity Commission Enforcement Guidance (2010). Policy Guidance on Current Issues of Sexual Harassment.

Retrieved from:
http://www.eeoc.gov/eeoc/publications/upload/currentissues.pdf

Remedial Actions Employers Can Take if a Sexual Harassment Complaint Has Occurred (EEOC, 2010)

- *Investigate promptly and thoroughly immediately after the complaint is received.*
- *Take immediate corrective/punitive action to end sexual harassment as promptly as possible following the investigation.*
- *Restore lost benefits and opportunities resulting from harassment to the target of the behavior as soon as possible following the investigation.*
- *Take disciplinary action against the offending supervisor or employee, ranging from reprimand to discharge, reflecting the **severity** and **persistence** of their conduct.*
- *Hold all witnesses to sexual harassment accountable to disciplinary actions if they do not report such behavior to the appropriate department or supervisor.*
- *Conduct follow-up inquiries with the victim and perpetrator to ensure the harassment has ended and the victim has not suffered retaliation.*
- *Ensure confidentiality and protection from retaliation for the victim and witnesses to the greatest extent possible by the employer and all parties involved.*

List 6. Equal Employment Opportunity Commission Enforcement Guidance (2010). Policy Guidance on Current Issues of Sexual Harassment.

Retrieved from:
http://www.eeoc.gov/eeoc/publications/upload/currentissues.pdf

Criteria for Sexual Harassment Claims (EEOC, 2014)

- *Employer must have 15 or more employees (if not subject to state laws).*

- *180 days to file a charge with EEOC (may be extended by state laws).*

- *Harassment doesn't have to be of sexual nature, and can include offensive remarks about a person's sex.*

- *The harasser can be the victim's supervisor, a supervisor in another department, a co-worker, or someone who is not employed by the employer.*

- *Complaints do not have to be reported to supervisors or the workplace before a charge is filed with EEOC.*

- *Teasing or other isolated incidents that are not very serious may constitute illegal harassment when it is so frequent or severe that it creates a hostile work environment or when it results in an adverse employment decision.*

List 7. Equal Employment Opportunity Commission Enforcement Guidance (2010). Policy Guidance on Current Issues of Sexual Harassment.

Retrieved from:
http://www.eeoc.gov/eeoc/publications/upload/currentissues.pdf

Sexual Harassment Explicit Policy Recommendations

- *A statement showing strong disapproval and everyone is responsible for the prevention and reporting of sexual harassing behaviors.*

- *Include U.S. definition of sexual harassment or gender discrimination found in title VII of the Civil Rights Act of 1964: "Sexual harassment includes unwelcome sexual advances, requests for sexual favors, and other verbal or physical conduct of a sexually harassing nature, when: (1) submission to the harassment is made either explicitly or implicitly a term or condition of employment; (2) submission to or rejection of the harassment is used as the basis for employment decisions affecting the individual; or (3) the harassment has the purpose or effect of unreasonably interfering with an individual's work performance or creating an intimidating, hostile, or offensive working environment."*

- *Include contact information for employee relations coordinator or HR Department head.*

- *If alleged harassment involves threats or physical harm to target, the alleged harasser can be suspended with pay when an investigation takes place at our organization. If investigation supports charges, alleged harasser may be terminated.*

- *If the investigation finds that the alleged harassment was brought falsely with malicious intent, the charging party may be subject to disciplinary sanctions, including termination.*
- *Include a statement saying that if the employee is dissatisfied with the employer's response to his/her complaint, he or she may contact the EEOC (or state's division of human rights) with contact information.*
- *Include zero tolerance statement such as:* "This Company/Organization will not tolerate discrimination or harassment based on race, sex, age, color, national origin, disability, or one's protected activity in the workplace. Federal and state laws also make these types of discrimination or harassment illegal."

List 8. List of items to include in company policy. Modified from the South Dakota Division of Human Rights, Department of Labor and Regulation.

Retrieved from:
https://dlr.sd.gov/humanrights/publications/samplesexualharassmentpolicy.pdf

Supporting Materials: Graphs and Figures

Figure 1

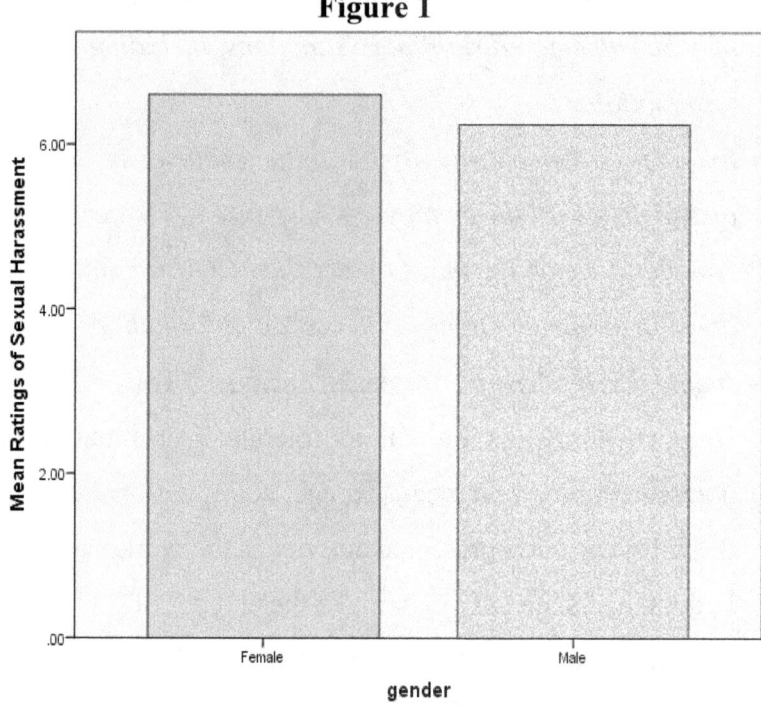

Figure 1. Gender differences in ratings of sexual harassment. Research has generally found that females tend to perceive the same behavior as sexual harassment more than males do. As seen here.

Figure 2

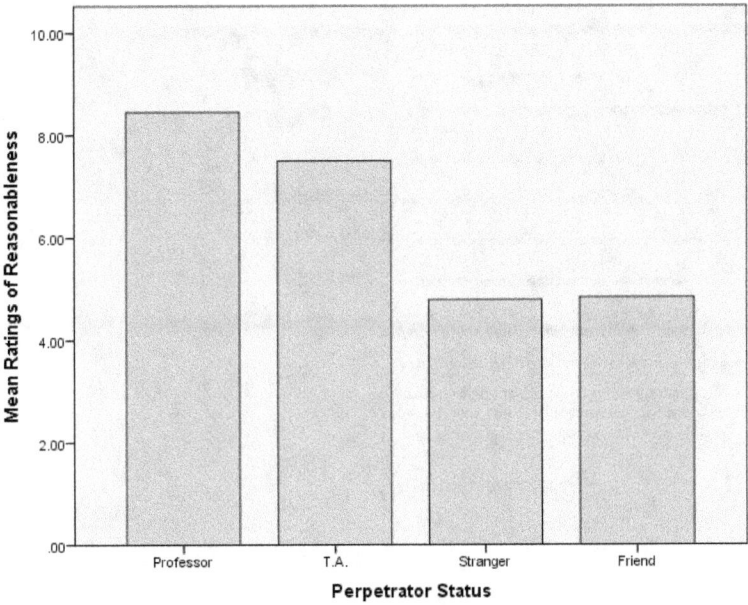

Figure 2. Perpetrator status differences in ratings of sexual harassment. Research has generally found that people are more likely to formally report sexual harassment when the perpetrator has some sort of formal power or authority over the target as opposed to no formal power or authority. For example, when the perpetrator is a student's professor or TA rather than a coworker or friend.

Figure 3

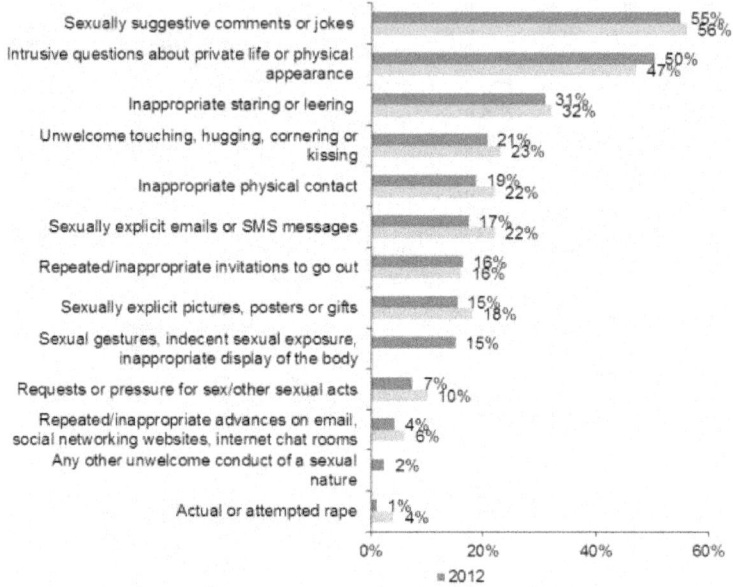

Figure 3. Results from a 2012 (compared to 2008) National Telephone Survey conducted by the Australian Human Rights Commission. The %age of women who experienced inappropriate behavior at work in 2012. Women most often experienced sexually suggestive comments or jokes (55%) inquisitive questions about their private life or physical appearance (50%) and inappropriate staring (31%). According to the survey, only 26.6% of targets reported experiencing unwanted physical behaviors in the past five years while 74.4% experienced unwanted verbal sexual conduct.

Figure 4

Women Harrassed At Workplace

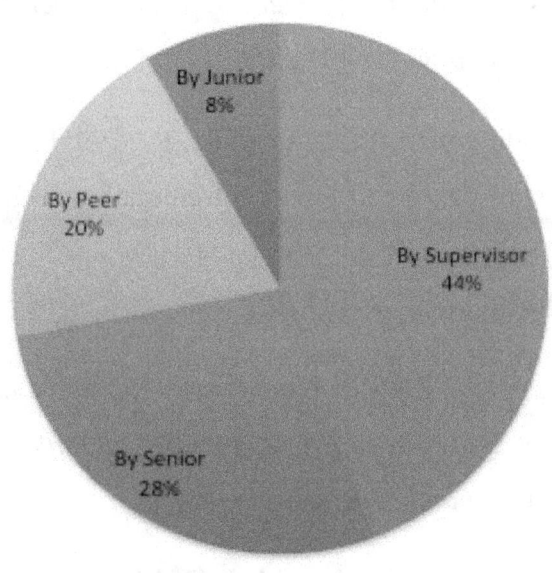

Figure retrieved from http://blog.9slides.com/wp-

content/uploads/2014/07/Screen-Shot-2014-07-31-at-2.08.52-PM.png

Figure 4. 2013 Survey conducted by The American Association of University Women (AAUW) measuring the source of sexual harassment. Of the women who reported they were sexually harassed, 72% reported they were harassed by either their direct supervisor (44%) or an employee that was senior to them (28%) (AAUW, 2013).

References

Abrams, D. (1998). Comments on the motivational status of self-esteem in social identity and intergroup discrimination. *European Journal of Social Psychology, 40*, 401–408.

Azy, B., Pitterman, Y., & Yitzhaki, R. (1995*).* An empirical test of the role of power differential in originating sexual harassment. *Basic and Applied Social Psychology, 17*, 497-517.

Bartling, C. A., & Eisenman, R. (1993). Sexual harassment proclivities in men and women. *Bulletin of the Psychonomic Society, 31*, 189-192.

Beasley, M. A., & Fischer, M. J. (2012). Why they leave: The impact of stereotype threat on the attrition of women and minorities from science, math and engineering majors. *Social Psychology of Education, 15*(4), 427-448.

Berdahl, J.L., Min, J.A. & Muradov, A.G. (2010) Modern treatment of discrimination: The gender mistreatment of women and gender role violators at work. *Psychology of Women Quarterly, 20*, 180-192.

Berdahl & Raver, (2012). Chapter: Sexual Harassment. APA Handbook of Industrial and Organizational Psychology, *American Psychological Association, 3*, 641-669.

Bowleg, L. (2008). When black + lesbian + woman ≠ black lesbian woman: The methodological challenges of qualitative and quantitative intersectionality research. *Sex Roles, 59*(5-6), 312-325.

Brescoll, V. Newman, G. Uhlmann, E. (2013). The Effects of System-Justifying Motives on Endorsement of Essentialist Explanations for Gender Differences. *Journal of Personality and Social Psychology, 105,* 891-908.

Bursik, K. (1992). Perceptions of sexual harassment in an academic context. *Sex Roles, 27,* 401-412.

Byars-Winston, A., Gutierrez, B., Topp, S., Carnes, M. (2011) Integrating theory and practice to increase scientific workforce diversity: A framework for career development in graduate research training. *CBE Life Science Education, 10,* 357–367.

Carli, L. (2004). Gender effects on persuasiveness and compliance gaining: A review. *Perspectives on persuasion, social influence and gaining,* 133-148.

Ceci, S. J. & Williams, W.M. (2011). Understanding Current Causes of Women's Underrepresentation in Science. *National Academy of Sciences, 108,* 792-799.

Chapman, T., Arnqvist, G., Bangham, J., Rowe, L. (2005). Sexual conflict trends and updates. *Ecol Evol, 18,* 41–47.

Cheung, F. M., & Halpern, D. F. (2010). Women at the top: Powerful leaders define success as work and family in a culture of gender. *American Psychologist, 65*(3), 182-193.

Clancy, K, Nelson, Rutherford, J, Hinde, K. (2014). *Survey of Academic Field Experiences (SAFE): Trainees Report Harassment and Assault.* doi:10.1371/journal.pone.0102172.

Dovidio, J., & Gaertner, S., (2010). Intergroup Bias. *Blackwell handbook of Social Psychology, 4,* 109-120.

Equal Employment Opportunity Commission Enforcement Guidance (2010). Policy Guidance on Current Issues of Sexual Harassment. Retrieved from: http://www.eeoc.gov/eeoc/publications/upload/curren tissues.pdf

Equal Employment Opportunity Commission Enforcement Guidance. EEOC Annual Report. (2015). Enforcement and litigation statistics. Retrieved from: http://www.eeoc.gov/eeoc/statistics/ enforcement/inde x.cfm.

Firestone, J.M., & Harris, R.J. (1994). Sexual harassments in the U.S. military: Individualized and environmental contexts. *Armed Forces and Society, 21*, 25-43.

Fisk, S. T., Cuddy, A. Glick, P. & Xu, J. (2002). A model of (often mixed) stereotype content: Competence and warmth respectively follow from perceived status and competition. *Journal of Personality and Social Psychology, 82,* 878-902.

Fitzgerald, O. (1991). Perceptions of sexual harassment: The influence of gender and academic context. *Psychology of Women Quarterly, 15,* 281-294.

Glick, P., & Fiske, S. T. (1999). Sexism and other "isms": Interdependence, status, and the ambivalent content of stereotypes., *Sexism and stereotypes in modern society,* 193-221.

Ilies, R., Hauserman, N., Schwochau, S., & Stibal, J. (2003). Reported incidence rates of work-related sexual harassment in the United States: Using meta-analysis to explain reported rate disparities. *Personnel Psychology, 56,* 607–631.

Jimeno-Ingrum, D., Berdahl, J. L., & Lucero-Wagoner, B. (2009). Stereotypes of Latinos and Whites: Do they guide evaluations in diverse work groups? *Cultural Diversity and Ethnic Minority Psychology, 15*(2), 158-164. Doi: 10.1037/a0015508.

Jobs DB Career Guide. (2014). The differences between the four types of Harassment. Job Seeker Handbook (2014). Retrieved from: http://my.jobsdb.com/MY/EN/V6HTML/JobSeeker/handbook/regulation-of- employment/sexual-harassment_3.htm.

Jost, J. T., Pelham, B. W., & Carvallo, M. (2002). Non-conscious forms of system justification: Cognitive, affective, and behavioral preferences for higher status groups. *Journal of Experimental Social Psychology, 38*, 586-602.

Jost, J. T., Banaji, M. R., & Nosek, B. A., (2004). A Decade of System Justification Theory: Accumulated Evidence of Conscious and Unconscious Bolstering the Status Quo. *Political Psychology, 25*, 883-918.

Kennelly. (1999). That Single Mother Element': How White Employers Typify Black Women. *Gender and Society, 13,*168-92.

Kowalewsk, O. (2009). Sexual Harassment. *MRK Health.* Retrieved from: https://mrkhealth.pbworks.com/w/pagerevisions/11953076/How%20can%20IA%20students%20recognize%20and%20prevent%20sexual%20harassment.

Marks, M. A., & Nelson, E. S. (1993). Sexual harassment on campus: Effects of professor gender on perception of sexually harassing behaviors. *Sex Roles, 28*, 207-217.

Mohipp, C., & Senn, C. (2008). Graduate students' perception of contra power sexual harassment. *Journal of Interpersonal Violence. 23*, 1258-1276.

Moss-Racusin, C., Dovidio, J. F., Brescoll, V. L., Graham, M. J., & Handelsman, J. (2012). Science faculty's subtle gender biases favor male students. *PNAS Proceedings of the National Academy of Sciences of the United States of America, 109*(41), 16474-16479.

Nosek, B. A., (2007). Pervasiveness and correlates of implicit attitudes and stereotypes. *European Review of Social Psychology, 18*, 36-88.

Pew Research Center, February, 2014, <u>Prevalence of Online Harassment in the United States</u>. Retrieved from: http://www.people-press.org/files/2015/01/1-8-15-Financial-security-release.pdf.

Rape Abuse and Incest National Network (RAINN). (2014). *Statistics on Sexual Assault*. Retrieved from: https://www.rainn.org/get-information/statistics/frequency-of-sexual-assault.

Raver, J. L. (2007). Sexual harassment vs. generalized workplace aggression: Construct differentiation and construct antecedents, *European Work and Organizational Psychology, 42*, 77-88.

Riegle-Crumb, C. & King, B. (2010). Questioning a white male advantage in STEM: Examining disparities in college major. *Educational Researcher, 39*, 656-664.

Rudmen, L., Ashmore, A., Gary, M., (2001) "Unlearning" automatic biases: The malleability of   implicit prejudice and stereotypes. *Journal of Social Psychology, 81*, 856-868.

Schein, E. H. (1985). *Organizational culture and leadership: A dynamic view.* San Francisco, CA: Jossey-Bass.

Schein, E. H. (1991). *What is culture?* In P. J. Frost, L. F. Moore, M. R. Louis, C. C. Lund-berg, & J. Martin (Eds.), Reframing organizational culture (pp. 243-253). Newbury Park, CA: Sage.

Sexual Harassment Handbook. *General Questions and Answers about Sexual Harassment: the Guide to the University of Pennsylvania's Sexual Harassment Policy.* (2014). University of Pennsylvania. Retrieved from: http://www.upenn.edu/affirm-action/introsh.html.

Shih, M., Pittinsky, T., & Ambady, N. (1999). Stereotype susceptibility: Identity salience and shifts in quantitative performance. *Psychological Science, 10,* 80–83.

SHRM Society for Human Resource Management. (2006). Workplace romance survey. SHRM/CareerJournal.com.

Sinclair, S., Hardin, C. D., & Lowery, B. S. (2006). Self-stereotyping in the context of multiple social identities. *Journal of Personality and Social Psychology, 90,* 529–542.

Siy, J. O., & Cheryan, S. (2013). When compliments fail to flatter: American individualism and responses to positive stereotypes. *Journal of Personality and Social Psychology, 104*(1), 87-102. doi:10.1037/a0030183.

Sniderman, P., Piazza, B. (1993). T. The Scare of Race. *American Journal of Sociology, 100,* 1351-1354.

South Dakota Division of Human Rights, Department of Labor and Regulation. (2014). Sample Sexual Harassment Policy. Retrieved from: https://dlr.sd.gov/humanrights/publications/samplesex ualharassmentpolicy.pdf

Steele, C., Aronson, J. (1995). Stereotype Threat and the Intellectual Test Performance of African Americans. *Journal of Personality and Social Psychology, 69,* 797-811.

Steinbugler, A. C., Press, J. E., & Johnson Dias, J. (2006). Gender, race and affirmative action operationalizing intersectionality in survey research. *Gender & Society, 20*(6), 805-825.

Steinpreis, R., Anders, K., Ritzke, D. (1999). The impact of gender on the review of the curricula vitae of job applicants and tenure candidates: A national empirical study. *Sex Roles, 41*:509–528.

Stockdale, Y. Visio, M. & Barta, L. 1999. The sexual harassment of men- Evidence for a broader theory of sexual harassment and sex discrimination. *Psychology, Public Policy, and Law, 5,* 630-664.

Thomson, R. (2014). Sexual Harassment at Work: Types of Sexual Harassment. Retrieved from http://employment.findlaw.com/employment-discrimination/sexual-harrassment-at-work.html.

Timmerman, G., & Bajema, C. (2000). The impact of
organizational culture on perceptions and Experiences
of sexual harassment. *Journal of Vocational
Behavior, 57,* 188-205.
http://dx.doi.org/10.1006/jvbe.1999.1741

Toossi, M. (2012). Labor force projections to 2020.
Monthly Labor Review, 135 (1), 43-64.

Trytten, D.A., Wong Lowe, A., & Walden, S.E. (2012).
"Asians are Good at Math. What an Awful
Stereotype": The Model Minority Stereotype's Impact
on Asian American Engineering Students, *Journal of
Engineering Education, 101*(3), 439-468.

U.S. Department of Education, National Center for
Education Statistics, Integrated Postsecondary
Education Data System (IPEDS), "Fall Staff Survey"
(IPEDS-S:91–99); and IPEDS Winter 2001–02
through Winter 2011–12, Human Resources
component, Fall Staff section. *Digest of Education
Statistics.*

U.S. Department of Justice. *National Crime
Victimization Survey.* 2009-2013.

U.S. Department of Justice. (2014). *Seasonal Patterns in
Criminal Victimization Trends.*

U.S. Department of Justice. (2013). *National Crime Victimization Survey*: 1993-2013.

U.S. Department of Labor, Bureau of Labor Statistics. (2012). *Occupational outlook handbook, Accountants and Auditors*:2012.

U.S. Equal Employment Opportunity Commission (1990), *Policy Guidance on Employer Liability under Title VII for Sexual Favoritism*. 29 C.F.R. § 1604.11. Title VII/EPA Division, Office of Legal Counsel.

Vasquez-Guignard, S. (2010). Latina university professors: insights into the journeys of those who strive to leadership within academia. Doctoral thesis, Pepperdine University, Malibu, California.

Williams, Elizabeth, Mary. (2011). Anthony Weiner: Why it's harassment. *Salon News*. Retrieved from: http://www.salon.com/2011/06/10/anthony_weiner_h arassment/

Willness, C. R., Steel, P. & Lee, K. (2007), A meta-analysis of the antecedents and consequences of workplace sexual harassment. *Personnel Psychology, 60*, 127– 162. doi: 10.1111/j.1744-6570.2007.00067.

Zadrozny, Brandy. (2014). Two Thirds of these female
scientists say they have been sexually harassed. *The
Daily Beast.*
http://www.thedailybeast.com/articles/2014/07/16/tw
o-thirds- of-these-female-scientists-say-they-ve-been-
sexually-harassed.html

About the Author

Ryan Jacobson is currently a Ph.D. student studying Industrial - Organizational Psychology at Florida International University. Ryan takes an applied approach to his research as well as his writing and takes pride in ensuring the content of his writing is applicable to organizational practice and is friendly to employers.

His main research interests include examining how organizational policies influence sexual harassment reporting behavior and employee attitudes in the workplace as well as using an intersectional perspective to examine perceptions of competence, the likelihood of being hired, and friendliness as a function of ethnicity and gender of the applicant. He is also interested in employee perceptions and organizational tolerance towards counterproductive behaviors and how such perceptions subsequently influence employment outcomes. These include organizational commitment, pro-social work behaviors, contextual performance, turn-over intentions, and job satisfaction, as well as the likelihood of reporting counterproductive workplace behaviors. Other research related interests include emotional intelligence, political skill, and the effectiveness of other predictors that can be used to measure job performance.

Through his applied experience as a consultant and his research experience analyzing organizational behavior as an I/O Ph.D. student, Ryan has developed a specialty for understanding employee behavior in organizations. He is seeking a future career as a professional as either an I/O psychologist Ph.D. consultant or a professor at a university.